Date: 6/5/12

J 629.892 BRA
Brasch, Nicolas.
Robots and artificial intelligence /

PALM BEACH COUNTY
LIBRARY SYSTEM
3650 SUMMIT BLVD.
WEST PALM BEACH, FL 33406

the Technology behind

ROBOTS AND ARTIFICIAL INTELLIGENCE

Nicolas Brasch

- Is It Possible to Create a Robot that Thinks and Acts Exactly Like a Human?
- Can Robots Perform Surgery?
- How Does Artificial Intelligence Work?

This edition first published in 2011 in the United States of America by Smart Apple Media. All rights reserved.
No part of this book may be reproduced in any form or by any means without written permission from the publisher.

Smart Apple Media
P.O. Box 3263
Mankato, MN, 56002

First published in 2010 by
MACMILLAN EDUCATION AUSTRALIA PTY LTD
15–19 Claremont St, South Yarra, Australia 3141

Visit our web site at www.macmillan.com.au or go directly to www.macmillanlibrary.com.au

Associated companies and representatives throughout the world.

Copyright © Nicolas Brasch

Library of Congress Cataloging-in-Publication Data

Brasch, Nicolas.
Robots and artificial intelligence / Nicolas Brasch.
p. cm. — (The technology behind)
Includes index.
ISBN 978-1-59920-569-4 (library bound)
1. Robots—Juvenile literature. 2. Robotics—Juvenile literature.
3. Artificial intelligence—Juvenile literature. I. Title
TJ211.2.B724 2011
629.8'9—dc22
2009054435

Publisher: Carmel Heron
Managing Editor: Vanessa Lanaway
Editor: Georgina Garner
Proofreader: Erin Richards
Designer: Stella Vassiliou
Page layout: Stella Vassiliou and Raul Diche
Photo researcher: Wendy Duncan (management: Debbie Gallagher)
Illustrators: Guy Holt, p. 12; Alan Laver, pp. 15, 26, 30; Richard Morden, p. 13; Karen Young, p. 1 and Try This! logo.
Production Controller: Vanessa Johnson

Manufactured in China by Macmillan Production (Asia) Ltd.
Kwun Tong, Kowloon, Hong Kong
Supplier Code: CP March 2010

Acknowledgements
The author and the publisher are grateful to the following for permission to reproduce copyright material:

Front cover photographs:
Microchip © edfuentesg/iStockphoto; Robot dog courtesy of photolibrary; Asimo © Shutterstock/Denis Klimov.

AAP Image/Art Gallery of New South Wales, **23** (left); AAP Image/Marine Nationale/Major Fromentin, **11** (left); © U.S.Navy/Science Faction/Corbis, **6** (top); © Ricardo Azoury/iStockphoto, **10** (top); © edfuentesg/iStockphoto, **7** (top); © Chris Schmidt/iStockphoto, **4**; © Borislav Toshev/iStockphoto, **5** (bottom); The Kobal Collection/20th Century Fox/LucasFilm, **7** (bottom); © Teun van den Dries/Photodisc/Getty Images, **14**; © Bill Ingalls/NASA/ Time & Life Pictures/Getty Images, **18** (top); © Junko Kimura/Getty Images, **9** (center); © Douglas McFadd/Getty Images, **27**; © Tom Mihalek/AFP/Getty Images, **26**; © MIT Media Lab/Getty Images, **18** (bottom); © John Mottern/ AFP/Getty Images, **9** (top); © Spencer Platt/Getty Images, **25** (top); © Wally Santana/Getty Images, **28** (right); © Space Frontiers/Hulton Archive/Getty Images, **19** (top); © Mark O. Thiessen/National Geographic/Getty Images, **19** (bottom); © Yoshikazu Tsuno/AFP/Getty Images, **11** (right), **31**; © Toru Yamanaka/AFP/Getty Images, **22** (top); The Kobal Collection/Paramount Television, **23** (right); The Kobal Collection/The Halcyon Company, **29**; Reproduced with kind permission from the LEGO® Group, 2009. LEGO, the LEGO logo and MINDSTORMS are trademarks of the LEGO Group. ©2009 The LEGO Group, **22** (center); Picture Media/Reuters/Kimberley White, **21**; photolibrary, **12**; photolibrary/Science Photo Library, **5** (top), **6** (bottom), **10**, (bottom), **16**, **17**, **20**; photolibrary/Volker Steger, **24**; Andy Russell, Monash University, **13**; The Shadow Robot Company, **9** (bottom); © Shutterstock/Denis Klimov, **8**, **25** (bottom); © Shutterstock/2jenn, **28** (left).

While every care has been taken to trace and acknowledge copyright, the publisher tenders their apologies for any accidental infringement where copyright has proved untraceable. Where the attempt has been unsuccessful, the publisher welcomes information that would redress the situation.

The publisher would like to thank Heidi Ruhnau, Head of Science at Oxley College, for her assistance in reviewing manuscripts.

Please note
At the time of printing, the Internet addresses appearing in this book were correct. Owing to the dynamic nature of the Internet, however, we cannot guarantee that all these addresses will remain correct.

Contents

What Is Technology? 4

The Technology Behind Robots and Artificial Intelligence 5

What Is a Robot? 6

How Do Robots Work? 8

What Types of Robots Have Already Been Invented? 10

Is It Possible To Create a Robot that Thinks and Acts Exactly Like a Human? 12

How Are Robots Used in Industry? 14

Can Robots Perform Surgery? 16

How Are Robots Used in Exploration and Space? 18

Do Robots Play or Fight? 20

What Is the Robot Hall of Fame? 22

What Is AI? 24

How Does Artificial Intelligence Work? 26

Are Robots and Artificial Intelligence Positive for Humanity? 28

What Does the Future Hold for Robots and Artificial Intelligence? 30

Index 32

Look out for these features throughout the book:

"Word Watch" explains the meanings of words shown in **bold**

"Web Watch" provides web site suggestions for further research

What Is Technology?

▲ People use technology every day, such as when they turn on computers. Technology is science put into action to help humans and solve problems.

> *We're changing the world with technology.*
>
> Bill Gates, founder of the Microsoft Corporation

The First Tools
One of the first examples of technology, where humans used their knowledge of the world to their advantage, was when humans began shaping and carving stone and metals into tools such as axes and chisels.

Technology is the use of **science** for practical purposes, such as building bridges, inventing machines, and improving materials. Humans have been using technology since they built the first shelters and lit the first fires.

Technology in People's Lives

Technology is behind many things in people's everyday lives, from lightbulbs to can openers. It has shaped the sports shoes people wear and helped them run faster. Cars, trains, airplanes, and space shuttles are all products of technology. Engineers use technology to design and construct materials and structures such as bridges, roads, and buildings. Technology can be seen in amazing built structures all around humans.

Technology is responsible for how people communicate with each other. Information technology uses scientific knowledge to determine ways to spread information widely and quickly. Recently, this has involved the creation of the Internet, and e-mail and file-sharing technologies. In the future, technology may become even more a part of people's lives, with the development of robots and artificial intelligence for use in business, in the home, and in science.

Word Watch

science knowledge that humans have gathered about the physical and natural world and how it works

The Technology Behind Robots and Artificial Intelligence

When many people think of robots and artificial intelligence (AI), they think of movies and fictional books—and they think of the future, not the present. What these people do not realize is that their world is already full of robots and AI.

Robots and AI in Everyday Life

Robots are part of people's lives in many ways. Robot toys entertain children, robot machines are responsible for making cars and chocolates, and robots even help perform surgery on sick people.

Artificial intelligence is part of people's lives, too. AI helps people book airline tickets **online**, wash their clothes in washing machines, make decisions about what books and CDs to buy, and it also helps police identify and catch criminals.

Attitudes to Robots and AI

People often disagree about robot and artificial intelligence technology. Some people believe that this technology is positive for humanity, but others are scared that robots and machines may one day take over the world!

▲ A boy plays with his robot dog. Robots can entertain us in our homes.

▶ A robot is used on an assembly line in a factory. Robots are used in many industries.

The People Behind the Technology

Many people with different jobs are behind the technology involved with robots and artificial intelligence.

Robotic Engineer Designing, testing, and manufacturing robots

Industrial Engineer Designing and **overseeing** the construction of **industry** equipment, such as robotic arms

Computer Scientist Designing hardware and software for computers and other technologies, such as artificial intelligence

Neuroscientist Studying how the human nervous system, including the brain, works

industry activities concerned with making goods to sell, often in factories

online connected to the Internet or the World Wide Web

overseeing supervising or watching over

What Is a Robot?

A robot is a machine that does **mechanical** work without "hands-on" assistance from a human. This does not mean that humans are not involved in making robots work—in fact, robots cannot operate without some assistance from humans.

Hard-Working Robots

The word "robot" was first used by Karel Capek, a Czech writer, in 1920. The word comes from the Czech word *robota*, which means "hard work" or "forced labor." "Robotics" is the word that describes the study of robots. It was first used by the writer Isaac Asimov in 1941.

Human Assistance

Robots can be controlled directly by a human using a remote control or by a set of instructions that a person has entered into a computer program. Robots that are controlled directly by humans are called manually controlled robots. Robots not controlled directly by humans are called **autonomous** robots.

Robots can undertake tasks that humans can do, but they do not have brains and cannot work alone. Robots with programmed instructions cannot change their own programming—a human must update it.

Why Humans Need Robots

Robots make humans' lives easier and safer. Robots can work in environments that humans find uncomfortable or even impossible to work in. They can search collapsed buildings for survivors, collect valuable information from inside volcanoes, and investigate other planets.

Robots do not get tired, very rarely make mistakes (once they have passed testing), and do not take vacations or get sick. They can work 24 hours a day, every day of the year.

Robots are very good for jobs that are repetitive, such as working on a production line. Robots can also move much larger and heavier items than humans can.

▲ Robots can be used for dangerous jobs, such as locating explosive devices.

◀ Robots can be used for jobs that require precise movements, such as surgery.

Word Watch

autonomous acting independently

mechanical related to machines, machinery, and physical work

Are Computers Robots?

Computers are not robots because they do not perform any mechanical work. However, every robot has some sort of computer inside it. The computer might be like one that children use at school, or it could be a **microprocessor** as small as a fingernail.

▶ A microprocessor acts like the central processing unit (CPU) of a computer.

▲ In the popular *Star Wars* films, R2-D2 and C-3PO are robots called droids. Science-fiction books and films often feature robots with human-like appearances.

Robots in Fiction

Robots have featured in many fictional books, television programs, and films. Among the most famous are:

- R2-D2 and C-3PO, two friendly robots from the *Star Wars* movies
- T-800, a robot assassin from the film *Terminator*
- Bender, a robot with several bad habits in the television program *Futurama*
- Hymie, a robot on the side of good, not evil, in the television program *Get Smart*
- Noo Noo, a vacuum cleaner robot in the television program *Teletubbies*

Word Watch

microprocessor very small controller that has an electronic circuit

Web Watch

robots.net

How Do Robots Work?

Robots are controlled by humans, either by remote control or by a program written by computer programmers. Some robots have common parts, but they may move in different ways.

The Parts of a Robot

Robots are built from various materials, but usually metals and plastics, depending on the jobs they have to perform and the conditions they have to work in. Most robots need to be **robust**, because they must work for many, many years.

Many robots have a movable body with individual parts. Depending on its work, a robot may have four **limbs**, like a human, or perhaps just one arm. Light and sound sensors provide robots with information about the environment around them, like a human's eyes and ears.

The robot equivalent of a human brain is its controller. The controller allows all the parts to work together. The controller may work by remote control or be operated directly by a human. With computer-programmed robots, instructions are stored in the robot's memory. They can be updated or completely changed by the programmer if circumstances change.

Word Watch

limbs arms or legs

robust strong and tough

ultrasonic involving sound that has a higher frequency than that which can be heard by humans

A camera often acts as a robot's eyes or records information that a human could not otherwise see. Some robots have more than one camera, giving them the ability to see in all directions.

A robot requires a power source. This robot uses a battery, but some robots plug directly into an electrical outlet.

Ultrasonic sensors act as a robot's ears. They detect if sound waves bounce off an object that is in the way.

◀ This robot has two arms and two legs like a human.

Web Watch

www.thetech.org/robotics/activities/index.html

www.spectrum.ieee.org/robotics/robotics-software/march-of-the-sandbots

How Robots Move

Robots move with the help of **actuators**. Examples of actuators are electric motors, **hydraulic pistons**, and **compressed** air systems. Attached to the actuators are the parts that the robot moves on, such as wheels, caterpillar tracks, legs, or rails. Each of these parts is designed to work well in different environments and on different surfaces.

- Wheels are particularly useful in small, enclosed spaces or on smooth surfaces.
- Caterpillar tracks are particularly useful in rough terrain and for climbing up stairs.
- Legs are particularly useful for robots that have to walk up slopes or over uneven ground.
- Rails are used when robots have to perform tasks speedily, without needing to move off a set course, such as on construction lines.

The Shadow Hand

One of the most demanding tasks for a robotics expert is creating a robotic hand that is a copy of a human hand. Each individual part of the robotic hand requires a tiny motor to drive it. These motors act like the nerves in a human hand.

▲ A robot on wheels moves easily on smooth surfaces.

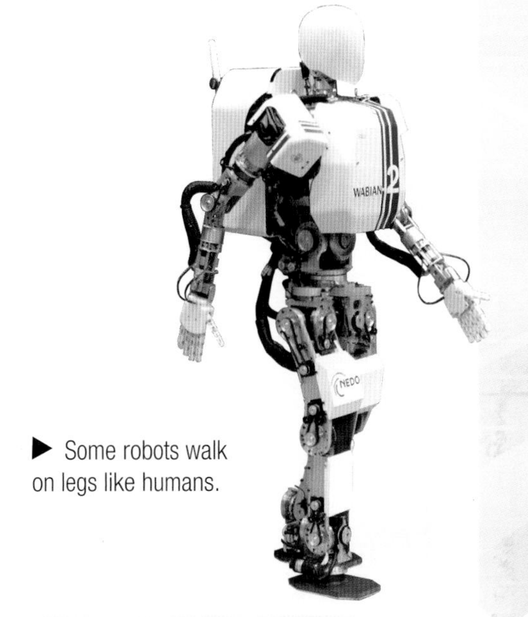

▶ Some robots walk on legs like humans.

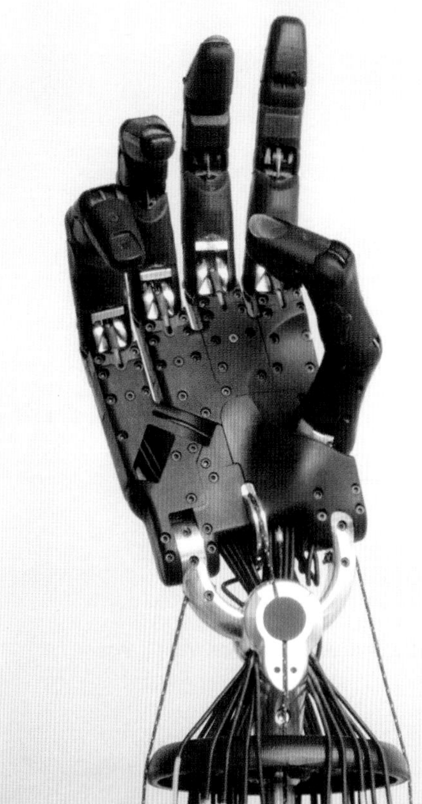

▶ The Shadow Hand is made by the Shadow Robot Company in the United Kingdom. It not only looks and moves like a human hand, it also picks up and handles objects with the same sensitivity as a human hand.

Animal Movements

Scientists build robots that copy human movements, such as walking and gripping, and researchers also study animals to see how they behave and move in certain environments. Sandbot, a robot that walks on sand, was designed to move like desert animals such as lizards.

Word Watch

actuators things that cause action, such as causing a machine to operate

compressed pressed together into a smaller space

hydraulic operated by liquid moving in a confined space under pressure

pistons cylinders that are pushed backward and forward by pressure

Web Watch

www.shadowrobot.com/hand

What Types of Robots Have Already Been Invented?

Robots may be used for exploration or for medical purposes, but the majority of robots are used in **industry**. Different types of robots are industrial robots, mobile robots, educational robots, agricultural robots, telerobots, and **humanoid** robots.

Industrial Robots

Industrial robots are generally used for work that is repetitive and requires accuracy, speed, and reliability. Many of the robots used in industry are robot arms.

▲ The car industry was the first to use robot arms on production lines.

A robot arm works in a similar way to a human arm. The area that the arm can move in is called its working envelope. This area is limited because the arm is fixed to a certain spot.

Robot arms have many joints so that they can move in many different directions. The directions in which a robot can move are known as degrees of freedom (DOF). Like a human elbow, a hinged arm has 1 DOF.

Mobile Robots

Mobile robots are also known as Automated Guided Vehicles (AGVs). They have wheels or legs that allow them to move independently. Mobile robots are used to carry equipment, explore an area of land, clean surfaces, and carry out various tasks that are non-repetitive and **nonsequential**.

Mobile robots that need to travel over smooth surfaces usually have small wheels, while those that work on rocky or uneven surfaces have large wheels or tracks. Mobile robots use light-sensitive sensors to follow lines on the floor or to detect when something is in their way. They also use pressure sensors so they know to move out of the way when they touch something.

▲ Automated Guided Vehicles transport car bodies to the next stage of an assembly line.

Human Versus Robot Workers

Industrial robots are often used to increase a company's **productivity** and **profit**. Unlike human workers, robot workers do not need to take breaks and do not need to be paid each week.

Unimate

The first industrial robot was Unimate, which was put into action at a General Motors plant in 1961.

Word Watch

humanoid looking and acting like a human

industry activities concerned with making goods to sell, often in factories

nonsequential not in a particular order

productivity amount of work done

profit amount of money made after costs have been taken out

Educational Robots

Educational institutions use robots to teach students how to design, program, build, and operate robots. One group of students sometimes competes against another to test which group has the best programming and operational skills.

Agricultural Robots

Agricultural robots do jobs such as plant seeds, pick fruit, and harvest crops. At the moment, few robots are used to do these tasks because the robots do not work as well or as fast as human workers.

Telerobots

Telerobots operate in locations that are dangerous to humans or where humans cannot go. Tiny telerobots swim through the body during microsurgery. Other robots travel to space. The arm of a space shuttle is a robot, performing maintenance tasks on satellites while being controlled by people known as teleoperators.

Oracle

A sheep-shearing robot, called Oracle, was developed by the University of Western Australia in 1979. It could move its clippers in six directions.

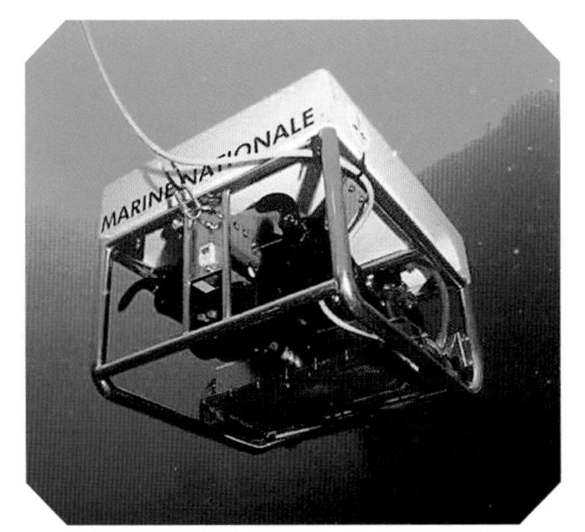

◀ A telerobot searches a deep-sea environment for plane wreckage.

▶ The humanoid robot HRP-4C was built to demonstrate voice recognition and speech technology. It sings along with piano music.

Humanoid Robots

Humanoid robots are used for research or for demonstration purposes. The most basic humanoids have a **torso**, two arms, two legs, and a head, and are able to walk when controlled by a human. Some researchers try to give robots the human senses of sight, hearing, and touch, and to get the robots to act and react in similar ways to humans.

Word Watch

torso main part of the body

Web Watch

www.inl.gov/adaptiverobotics/humanoidrobotics/whatis.shtml

prime.jsc.nasa.gov/ROV/types.html

kernow.curtin.edu.au/www/Agrirobot1/oracle.htm

Is It Possible to Create a Robot that Thinks and Acts Exactly Like a Human?

Humans think, **reason**, act, and react in ways that other animals do not. Robots with some human senses have been created, but the human brain is so complicated, it seems impossible to create a robot that would think and act exactly like a human.

Wetware, Hardware, and Software

Biological brains, such as the brains of humans and animals, are sometimes called wetware. This distinguishes them from silicon chips, called hardware, and programs, called software.

Thinking Like a Human

It would be a huge task for a robotics expert to create a robot that thinks and acts exactly like a human.

The Human Brain

The human brain is made up of nerve cells called **neurons**. There are about 100 billion neurons in a human brain. These neurons exchange electrochemical signals that determine how humans act, react, behave, and think.

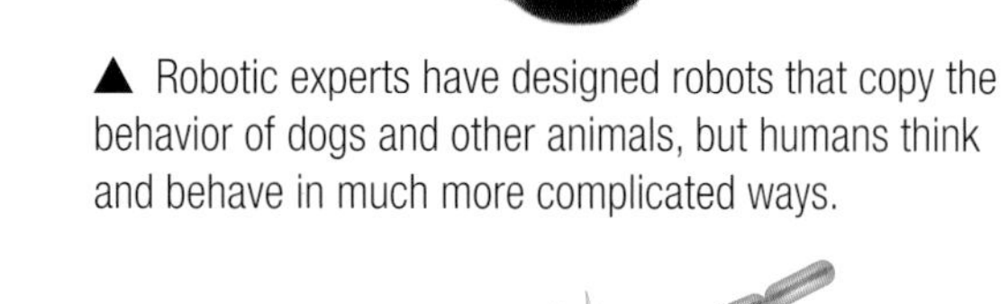

▲ Robotic experts have designed robots that copy the behavior of dogs and other animals, but humans think and behave in much more complicated ways.

▶ Each neuron has a small cell body with long extensions called axons and dendrites. The ends of the axons in one neuron meet the ends of the dendrites of other neurons. The neurons form an ever-changing **network**.

dendrites
neuron
axon
neuron
myelin covering
electrochemical signal

Word Watch

autonomous acting independently

ethical to do with what is right or wrong

network group or system of things that are connected

neurons cells that transmit nerve impulses as electrochemical signals

reason think, understand, and form judgements, considering all the facts and possibilities

Making Ethical Decisions

A robot cannot make **ethical** decisions like a human. A robot could be controlled or programmed to use a knife to kill a human—and it could not override its instructions or decide that this action was ethically wrong. The robot is controlled by humans and the humans who program it make decisions for the robot, deciding what they think is right and what is wrong.

An **autonomous** robot could be programmed to always protect human life, and it could base its work and decisions around this instruction. However, if the robot needed to make a decision, such as whether to save the lives of two children or two older people, it would come to its decision in a very different way from a human being.

Web Watch

faculty.washington.edu/chudler/cells.html

Behaving Like a Human

Many **humanoid** robots seem to touch, see, hear, and walk like humans, but they do not behave exactly like humans—yet.

The Human Senses

Humans have five senses, which are touch, hearing, sight, smell, and taste. Robots may use:

- pressure sensors to "touch"
- light sensors and cameras to "see"
- sonar sensors to "hear"

In these areas, robots can be just as sensitive as humans or even more so.

Touch, hearing, and sight have been developed because they are the most useful senses for robots. Spending time and money on developing robots with the senses of taste and smell has not been considered worthwhile.

More than Five Senses

One advantage that robots have over humans is that they are not limited to five senses. A robot fitted with a special camera and a heat sensor can tell how hot something is just by looking at it. This is very useful when fighting fires, because a robot can stand in front of a closed door, determine whether there is a fire behind the door and, if so, how hot the fire is.

▼ An Australian researcher, Andy Russell, has developed this robot, which can detect smells. A robot with a sense of smell could one day replace sniffer dogs at airports.

Balance and Walking

Robotics experts have designed and built robots that walk on two legs, but the robots cannot move as well as humans can. Unlike humans, they do not have the sensitive balancing process used by the brain and ears.

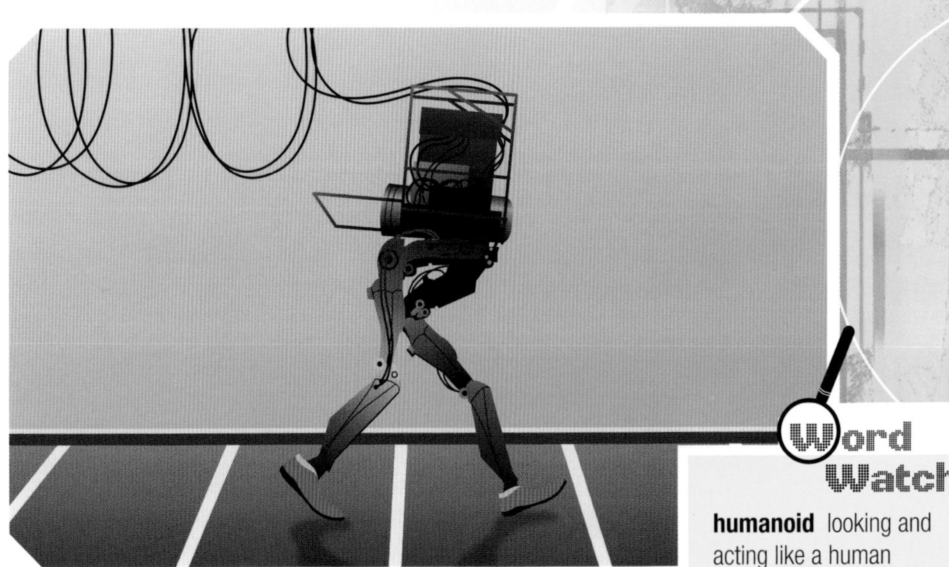

▶ A humanoid robot does not walk exactly like a human.

Word Watch

humanoid looking and acting like a human

How Are Robots Used in Industry?

Some **industrial** robots lift things that are too heavy for humans, some perform work that requires a high level of accuracy, and others work in environments that humans cannot work in. Industrial robots also do work that has to be repeated over and over and over again.

Hazardous Jobs
Some of the most hazardous and difficult jobs done by humans are on offshore oil rigs. These rigs stand in the ocean and are pelted by waves, wind, and rain. Technology is being developed that may see these offshore platforms run by robots alone, with humans operating them from land, many miles away.

Advantages of Robots in Industry

The main advantages of using robots in industry are that robots can perform certain tasks more quickly, easily, cheaply, and efficiently than human workers. They can also perform these tasks without a break—except for repairs and maintenance.

Heavy-Lifting Jobs

Robots are used for heavy lifting at Rotterdam Docks in the Netherlands. Rotterdam is the largest port in Europe. Instead of human dockworkers, who drive forklifts and cranes to lift containers on and off cargo ships, Rotterdam Docks uses more than 68 robot cranes and 140 robot trucks.

▲ Robot trucks carry containers from a ship at Rotterdam Docks. The robot trucks and cranes handle more than 12 million containers a year.

Word Watch

industrial to do with activities concerned with making goods to sell, often in factories

Small, Complicated Jobs

Robots created by the Bosch Group, called Delta robots, pack more than 40,000 chocolates an hour. They can:

- move and pick up the delicate chocolates
- recognize different types of chocolates
- position the chocolates in the chocolate box
- wrap some of the chocolates in paper wrapping

Among the features built into the Delta robots are:

- cameras to recognize each type of chocolate
- software that defines which robots pick up which chocolates and where they put the chocolates
- a communication unit that enables the robots to "communicate" with each other

Strong Robots

The world's largest six-axes industrial robot can lift weights of 2,600 pounds (1,200 kg) more than 20 feet (6 m) in the air. It is designed for lifting truck, tractor, and car parts.

Robots with Six Axes

One feature that many industrial robots have in common is that they have six **axes**.

Axis 4 allows the robot to make a move known as a wrist roll. It rotates the upper arm in a circular motion.

Axis 3 allows the robot's upper arm to rise and fall.

Axis 6 is responsible for a twisting motion in the robot's arm. It enables the arm to rotate freely in a circular motion.

Axis 5 allows the wrist of the robot to tilt up and down. Axis 4 and axis 5 movements often work together.

Axis 2 allows the lower arm of this robot to move forward and backward.

Axis 1 allows the robot to rotate from left to right. This means the robot's work area can be in front of the robot, as well as to either side of and behind the robot.

▶ A six-axes robot has a great deal of flexibility in its movement.

axes imaginary lines around which a body turns or rotates (singular: axis)

Can Robots Perform Surgery?

One of the greatest achievements in robotics has been the creation of robots that can be used in the field of medicine. Robots can help in surgery or perform surgery by themselves. They can also support humans as artificial **limbs** and as thought-controlled wheelchairs.

Telesurgery

Telesurgery sometimes involves the use of robots. Telesurgery is when a surgeon in one location **oversees** a surgical procedure taking place in a different location. The chief surgeon follows the progress of the surgery onscreen. Sometimes, the robots act directly on the instructions of the chief surgeon. Other robots are operated by surgeons at the scene of the surgery, instructed by the chief surgeon.

Robotic Surgery

Robots have been used in surgery since the 1980s. Early on, they only performed simple procedures, such as inserting needles into delicate parts of the human body. There are two main types of robotic surgery: independent and shared.

Independent Robotic Surgery

Independent robotic surgery involves a robot performing a procedure without the direct assistance of a surgeon. This can only be done after the robot has been programmed to carry out particular procedures in very specific ways. If something unexpected happens, the robot cannot change what it is doing, so its work is carefully supervised by a surgeon.

Shared Robotic Surgery

Shared robotic surgery involves a surgeon using a robot to help perform particularly complicated and time-consuming procedures. Shared robotic surgery often involves the use of a robot with cameras fitted to it, so that the robot can provide images from inside the body to the surgeon.

limbs arms or legs

oversees supervises or watches over

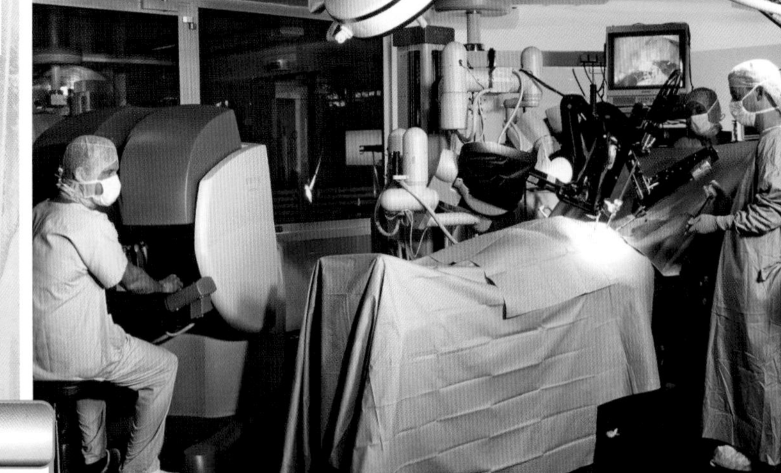

◀ In shared robotic surgery, the surgeon uses the robot much like other medical tools, except that the robot is more efficient and reliable.

Web Watch

www.cts.usc.edu/rsi-davincisystem.html

Robotic Limbs

Artificial limbs are built by robotics experts. Robotic limbs can look very different from human limbs and perform very complex tasks.

The key to developing robotic limbs has been understanding and copying the electrochemical messages sent by **neurons** in the human brain (see page 12) to various parts of the body. The physical and brain movements of the patient are monitored, then a computer chip is programmed and placed inside the robotic limb. The computer acts the same way as the patient's brain, causing the limb to move.

Thought-Controlled Robots

A robotic wheelchair has been developed that enables people with very little or no movement to use their thought processes to move their wheelchairs. The wheelchair scans the area around the chair and creates a **three-dimensional** picture that is displayed on a screen. The user wears a special cap with **electrodes**. The user concentrates on the part of the display where he or she want to move to. The electrodes pick up the signal from the user's brain and transmit it to the chair, which then moves to this spot.

Robot Nurses

Robot nurses can perform basic tasks such as carrying trays, understanding particular instructions, helping elderly people get around, and even delivering programmed amounts of drugs. They are not designed to replace human nurses, but they can help where there are shortages of nurses.

▶ A man adjusts his artificial robotic knee and leg.

Word Watch

electrodes parts of an electrical system that send and receive signals

neurons cells that transmit nerve impulses as electrochemical signals

three-dimensional using length, width, and depth

How Are Robots Used in Exploration and Space?

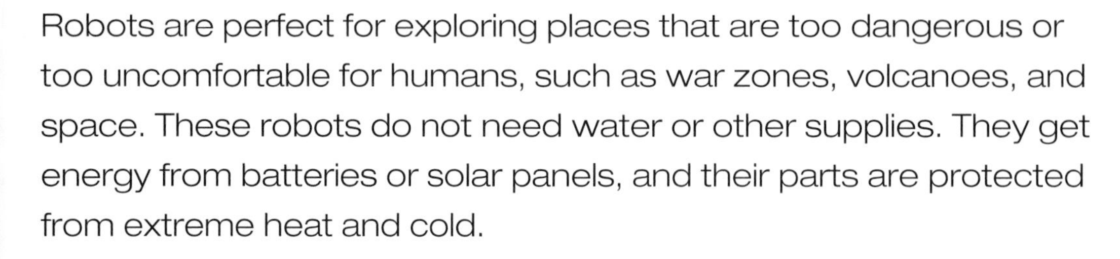

Robots are perfect for exploring places that are too dangerous or too uncomfortable for humans, such as war zones, volcanoes, and space. These robots do not need water or other supplies. They get energy from batteries or solar panels, and their parts are protected from extreme heat and cold.

Hot and Cold Conditions
The Nomad Rover is a robot that is used to study conditions in hot, dry desert environments and in icy areas. In 2000, it collected and **analyzed** meteorite samples across Antarctica.

Robot Exploration

Robots have been used to explore war zones, volcanoes, deep-sea areas, and even inside the pyramids of Egypt.

▶ The Afghan Explorer has a flat-screen monitor and can be used to conduct two-way interviews.

War Zones

A robot in Afghanistan goes where war correspondents are unable to go. The Afghan Explorer was designed by a computing and robotics expert who thought that people should know what is going on in dangerous war zones. It has been described as a cross between a lawn mower and a robotic dog.

Volcanoes

Robots can climb into volcanoes to collect gas samples and take photographs. Using robots means that **volcanologists** can avoid dangerous gases and high temperatures and do not need to risk their lives inside volcanoes.

The Deep Sea

Robots study life in deep-sea areas. Deep Drone 8000 can reach depths of 8,000 feet (2,500 m) below the ocean surface. Its movements are operated from the surface, although depth and direction are programmed into the robot before it descends. It has four cameras.

Pyramids of Egypt

A small robot named Pyramid Rover explored down a narrow shaft and drilled through a closed door in the Great Pyramid of Cheops. The robot inserted a camera into the drilled holes so that the images could be studied by **Egyptologists**.

▶ Dante II is a robot with eight legs that has collected vital information inside volcanoes.

Word Watch

analyzed examined something in detail
Egyptologists people who study ancient Egypt
volcanologists people who study volcanoes

Robots in Space

In space, robots can be used to explore places where humans cannot survive and also to operate and check spacecraft.

Rovers

In 1996–97, the Sojourner Rover robot was taken to the planet Mars by the *Mars Pathfinder* spacecraft. For its first few days on Mars, it was remotely operated from Earth. After that, it made its own decisions about the direction and distance it would travel by analyzing the ground it was on.

▶ The Sojourner Rover sent information about Mars's atmosphere, climate, and structure back to Earth. Since then, other rovers have been sent to Mars.

Stuck in the Sand

In April 2005, a rover on Mars got stuck in a sand dune. The operators on Earth tried for a month to free the rover, but without success. It eventually freed itself and continued exploring the planet, collecting samples, and sending back images.

Robot Astronaut

The Robonaut is a **humanoid** robot developed by the National Aeronautics and Space Administration (NASA), the organization in charge of the U.S. space program. It has been designed to undertake many of the tasks currently done by human astronauts in space. Robonaut can withstand very cold and very hot temperatures, as well as a lack of oxygen, and still perform its functions.

humanoid looking and acting like a human

Robot Checks

The AERCam Sprint is a robot that flies around the outside of space stations looking for faults. It looks like a large soccer ball and is fitted with two television cameras. The footage it takes is relayed back to Earth where it is examined. It is also fitted with 12 small nitrogen-gas-powered thrusters that propel it slowly around the space station.

▶ Robonaut is controlled by an astronaut or robotics expert. It sends back information from its cameras and sensors.

Web Watch

robonaut.jsc.nasa.gov/sub/hands.asp

spaceflight.nasa.gov/station/assembly/sprint/index.html

Do Robots Play or Fight?

Robots can be programmed for our fun and amusement. We can make them play soccer, and we can make them fight each other! But even when robots are designed for fun, the technology used to create them contributes a great deal to the field of robotics.

RoboCup Around the World

RoboCup has been held in a different city each year since 1997. Nagoya, Paris, Stockholm, Melbourne, Seattle, Lisbon, Osaka, and Atlanta have all hosted the tournament.

RoboCup

RoboCup involves groups of robotics experts building robots that then compete against each other in games of soccer. The ultimate aim is to "develop a team of fully **autonomous humanoid** robots that can play and win against the human world champion soccer team" by 2050.

▲ A robot prepares for a humanoid robot league game.

RoboCup Leagues

Robotics experts use their technological knowledge to build robots to compete in different leagues or levels.

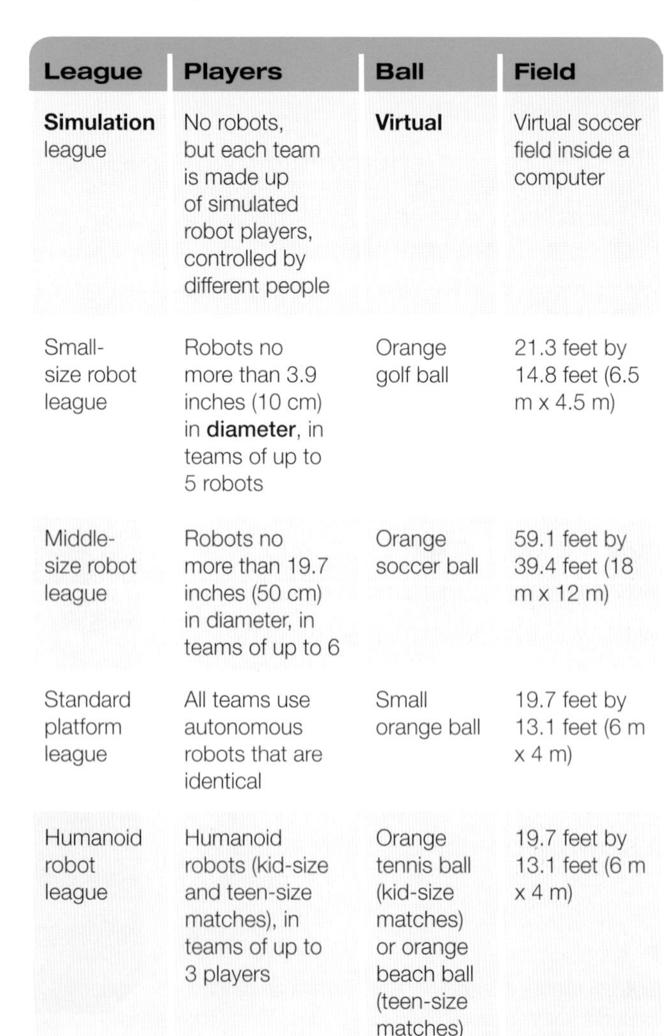

League	Players	Ball	Field
Simulation league	No robots, but each team is made up of simulated robot players, controlled by different people	**Virtual**	Virtual soccer field inside a computer
Small-size robot league	Robots no more than 3.9 inches (10 cm) in **diameter**, in teams of up to 5 robots	Orange golf ball	21.3 feet by 14.8 feet (6.5 m x 4.5 m)
Middle-size robot league	Robots no more than 19.7 inches (50 cm) in diameter, in teams of up to 6	Orange soccer ball	59.1 feet by 39.4 feet (18 m x 12 m)
Standard platform league	All teams use autonomous robots that are identical	Small orange ball	19.7 feet by 13.1 feet (6 m x 4 m)
Humanoid robot league	Humanoid robots (kid-size and teen-size matches), in teams of up to 3 players	Orange tennis ball (kid-size matches) or orange beach ball (teen-size matches)	19.7 feet by 13.1 feet (6 m x 4 m)

Word Watch

autonomous acting independently

diameter straight line that passes from one side of a figure to the other, passing through the center

humanoid looking and acting like a human

simulation computer model or something else that pretends to be real

virtual computer image that seems to exist, but does not really exist

Robot Battles

Robot battles promote **innovation** in robotics technology. BattleBots hosts battles between robots and shows the battles on its television show.

BattleBots

In a BattleBots contest, one robot tries to defeat another robot, like competitors in a boxing match. Like boxers, robots compete against other robots that are of the same weight. A boxer stands on a set of scales and has his or her whole body weighed before a fight, but a BattleBots robot has each of its segments weighed separately and then all the segment weights are added up.

Robots must have at least one weapon system. The weapon system either takes control of the other robot by lifting or grabbing it or causes damage through direct physical contact, such as by using hammers, flippers, or spinners. Robots may also be fitted with mechanisms that produce flames or smoke. This just adds to the excitement of the battle!

Robot Rumbles
Apart from one-on-one robot contests, BattleBots also holds Robot Rumbles, which involve several robots fighting each other at once.

innovation
introduction of new ideas and new ways to do things

▲ A BattleBots contest takes place in an arena that is about 47.6 feet by 47.6 feet (14.5 m × 14.5 m). Robots are remotely controlled from outside the arena. Autonomous robots are not allowed.

Web Watch

www.robocup.org
www.battlebots.com

What Is the Robot Hall of Fame?

The Robot Hall of Fame honors real robots and also fictional robots that have inspired breakthroughs in robotics technology. Every year, up to five robots are **inducted** into the Robot Hall of Fame.

Recognizing Robot Excellence

The Robot Hall of Fame was created by Carnegie Mellon University in the United States in 2003. It recognizes excellence in robotics technology all around the world.

Robots from Science

The category "Robots from **Science**" refers to robots that were built for scientific purposes. Among the inductees in this category are:

- Sojourner Rover, which explored Mars in 1997 (see page 19)
- Unimate, which was the first industrial robot. It joined the assembly line at a General Motors car plant to work with **die-casting** machines in 1961
- ASIMO, which is a **humanoid** robot unveiled in 2000 that was the result of 15 years of research by the Honda Motor Company
- Shakey, which is the first mobile robot that can **reason**. It was developed by the Stanford Research Institute in the United States in the late 1960s.
- AIBO, which was introduced in Japan in 1998. It was the first robot designed to be sold for personal use.
- SCARA, which was created in 1978. It revolutionized the design of robot arms used on small electronic assembly lines.
- Raibert Hopper, which was used to study robotic motion, particularly in walking robots
- LEGO Mindstorms, which is a robotics toolset that people can use to experiment and have fun in the field of robotics

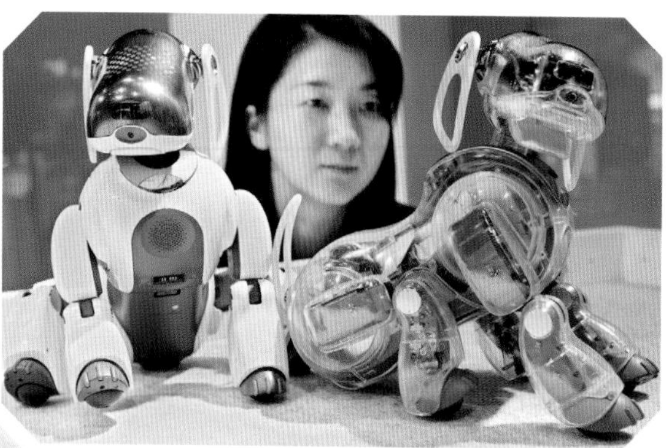

▶ In English, AIBO stands for Artificial Intelligence BOt. In Japanese, it sounds like the word "companion."

▶ This robot was created using a LEGO Mindstorms toolset.

Word Watch

die-casting pouring liquid metal into molds

humanoid looking and acting like a human

inducted admitted formally into a club or group

reason think, understand, and form judgements, considering all the facts and possibilities

science knowledge that humans have gathered about the physical and natural world and how it works

Robots from Science Fiction

The category "Robots from Science Fiction" refers to fictional robots that have appeared in films, books, or other media. Among the inductees in this category are:

- HAL 9000, a computer that acts as the brain of the spaceship *Discovery* in the film *2001: A Space Odyssey*
- R2-D2, a 3.15-foot (0.96-m) tall robot that helps Luke Skywalker in the *Star Wars* films
- Astro Boy, a comic book and television character created in Japan in 1951
- Robby the Robot, a charming, funny robot that delighted audiences in the 1956 film *Forbidden Planet*
- Maria, a humanoid robot from the 1927 German film *Metropolis*
- Lieutenant Commander Data, a character from the *Star Trek: Next Generation* series

▲ In Japan, Astro Boy is known as Mighty Atom. He has been described as the first robot with a soul.

▲ Lieutenant Commander Data has raised questions about what it means to be a robot and what it means to be human.

Arthur C. Clarke
Arthur C. Clarke was one of the world's most famous science fiction writers. He was among the judges of the Robot Hall of Fame until his death in 2008.

Try This!

Nominate a Robot

You can nominate a robot for the Robot Hall of Fame by following these steps.

1. Think of a robot that you would like included in the Robot Hall of Fame. Perhaps ask your classmates for their ideas as well.
2. Go to www.robothalloffame.org and check if your suggestion is already in the Hall of Fame. If it is, try to think of another worthy entry.
3. If your suggestion is not in the Hall of Fame, click on the "Nominate a Robot" link and nominate your entry.

www.robothalloffame.org

What Is AI?

Artificial intelligence (AI) is a branch of computer **science** that aims to program machines to think and learn by themselves, in the same way that humans think and learn. One example of artificial intelligence used today is facial recognition systems.

Human Intelligence

To gain an understanding of artificial intelligence, it is necessary to understand what human intelligence is. Intelligence describes the way humans learn things and how they apply their knowledge and skills in different situations, through their actions and behavior. Intelligence involves learning from past experiences so that the right decisions can be made in the future. Decisions are not only based on what has happened in the past, but also on the slightly different circumstances and conditions that are present now.

Word Watch

science knowledge that humans have gathered about the physical and natural world and how it works

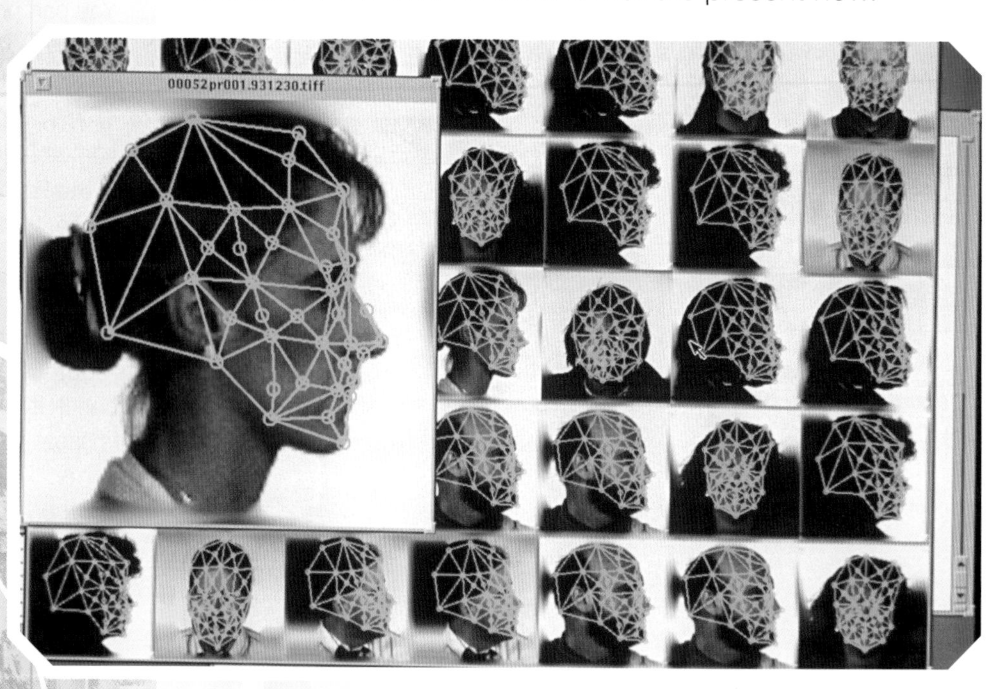

◀ A facial recognition system is one form of artificial intelligence. It can "learn" by gathering data and it can apply this knowledge to make decisions.

History of Artificial Intelligence

Research into artificial intelligence began in the 1940s, soon after the first computers were developed. Computer scientists identified similarities between the human brain and the computer. Some scientists thought that by gaining an understanding of how humans make decisions, computers could be made to act in the same way.

In 1956, a US computer scientist named John McCarthy coined the phrase "artificial intelligence" for the idea that machines could learn like humans do. Since the 1950s, this area of science has become more and more successful.

Web Watch

world.honda.com/ASIMO

www.ai.mit.edu/projects/sociable/overview.html

Types of Artificial Intelligence

There are two types of artificial intelligence: expert systems and learning systems. Expert systems have all the knowledge required to solve a problem. Learning systems recognize patterns and make decisions based on these patterns.

Expert Systems

The knowledge in expert systems is input by humans. The systems do not have to access or process other information. An example is an airline flight booking system. Customers type in the cities they wish to fly between and the dates they wish to fly. The booking system then matches this information with the information it already has in its program and comes up with available flights.

Learning Systems

Learning systems recognize patterns or changes in patterns, rather than precise information. Examples are credit card fraud, handwriting recognition, and facial recognition systems.

▲ A handwriting recognition system is a learning system that can convert handwriting into typed words.

ASIMO

ASIMO is a **humanoid** robot with very advanced artificial intelligence. It has the ability to:

- detect the distance and direction of objects that are within view of its camera or sensors
- recognize human **postures** and **gestures** and respond to them
- recognize and deal with the physical features of its environment
- distinguish sounds, including certain words, and respond to them
- recognize some people's faces

▲ ASIMO can recognize humans and respond to them.

Logic Theorist

The first artificial intelligence program was the Logic Theorist, developed by Allen Newell and Herbert Simon in the 1950s. A tree represented a problem that the program had to solve. The computer program would choose a branch that would most likely result in the best outcome and it would slowly move up the tree toward the correct answer. It chose the branches using the rules and **reasoning** that Newell and Simon had given it.

Word Watch

gestures movements of parts of people's bodies, such as the way they move their hands

humanoid looking and acting like a human

postures positions of people's bodies, such as the way they stand or sit

reasoning thinking, understanding, and forming judgements, considering all the facts and possibilities

How Does Artificial Intelligence Work?

Complex **neuron networks** in the brain provide humans with intelligence. Artificial intelligence researchers build artificial neural networks so that computers can work like human brains.

Turing Test
The Turing Test determines the intelligence of a machine. An examiner asks questions of a human and a computer, without knowing which is which. If the examiner is unable to tell the two apart, then the machine is said to be intelligent.

Artificial Neural Networks

Artificial neural networks are formed with millions of tiny electronic processing units connected by wires. A network is trained by giving it information to process, called inputs, as well as the associated answer, called the output. The network processes the inputs over and over until it gets an answer that is the same as the output. In a human brain, scientists call this process learning.

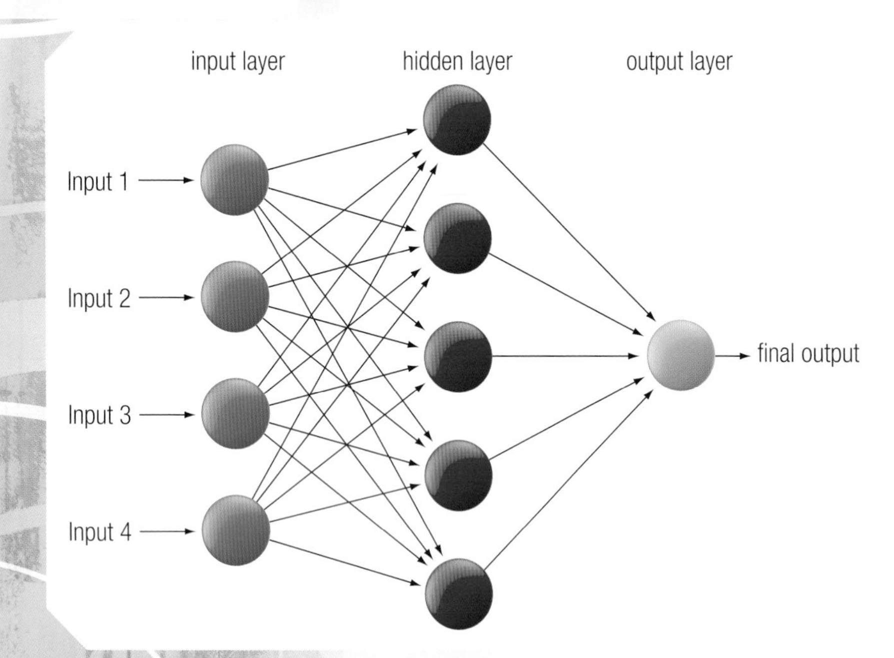

▲ An AI program operates on the input until it finds an answer that matches the output. Humans learn in this way too, using a process called trial and error.

Intelligent Computers

Intelligent computers are built from the top down or the bottom up. The top-down approach copies the way the human brain works. Lots of input is provided and the computer examines the relationships between the input, or what it "knows," before coming up with a solution. A top-down computer can be programmed to play chess. It is provided with rules and strategies and it processes and **analyzes** each move when playing a game.

The bottom-up approach involves copying the physical development of the human brain. When humans are born, they have small brains, little understanding, and little knowledge. Over time, the amount of information in the brain increases, as does the ability to understand and solve problems. Bottom-up computers start with a simple program that is able to learn by itself, adding to its own knowledge base.

▲ Deep Blue, a computer developed by IBM, beat the world chess champion Gary Kasparov in a series of matches in 1997. Chess computers use the top-down approach to AI.

Word Watch

analyzes examines something in detail

networks groups or systems of things that are connected

neuron cell that transmits nerve impulses as electrochemical signals

Everyday Uses of Artificial Intelligence

Examples of artificial intelligence can be seen in everyday life. AI can help people wash, vacuum, pay their bills, and choose books **online**.

Washing Machines

Some washing machines use "fuzzy **logic**" to control their water level, water temperature, wash time, amount of detergent, and spin speed. Decisions are based on the conditions that their sensors pick up, such as the amount of dirty clothes in the machine.

Voice Recognition Software

Voice recognition software is used by call centers to answer phone calls, respond to queries, and perform tasks without human involvement. The best voice recognition systems do not just understand words, they understand which words go together, like "pay" and "bill." This is called natural language processing.

Shopping Online

Many retail companies use artificial intelligence to improve their customers' shopping experience—and to boost sales. Amazon.com records a customer's book or CD purchases, then recommends other books and CDs that the customer might like to buy.

◀ The Roomba vacuum cleaner cleans a room by itself. Its sensors detect when it is near a wall or furniture, and it can be programmed to return to its base when finished.

▶ Amazon.com bases its book and CD recommendations on what similar customers have bought.

Credit Card Fraud

Banks use artificial intelligence technology to try to stop credit card fraud. They create a profile of a customer's card use and buying habits. An artificial intelligence system notices if the pattern of use changes, such as large purchases being made in a different country. The bank then contacts the customer or cancels the credit card.

Word Watch

logic system of reasoning, which involves thinking, understanding, and forming judgements, considering all the facts and possibilities

online connected to the Internet or the World Wide Web

Are Robots and Artificial Intelligence Positive for Humanity?

There are some people who claim that robots and artificial intelligence will greatly benefit humankind—and others who claim they will harm our way of life.

Robots in the Military
There are about 4,000 robots "serving" in the U.S. military. They perform tasks such as looking for roadside bombs in Iraq and Afghanistan. Some people argue that this is positive for humanity because robots are put at risk, not humans. Some people argue that this is negative for humanity, because armed robots can be just a new way of killing people.

The Argument Against Robots

Ever since the first robots were created, a large concern has been that robots take jobs away from humans. Robots can perform without a break, unless they need repairing, and do not need to be paid every week. People argue that business owners will replace their work forces with robots, and many people will lose their jobs. Another argument against robots is that they may become so advanced that one day they will be able to take over the world.

The Argument For Robots

Other people argue that new jobs are created because robots have to be built, programmed, and maintained. Robots can also make life a lot easier for humans by doing jobs that humans are unwilling or unable to do. When used in the field of medicine, robots can save lives.

▼ A soldier uses a remote-controlled robot to search for mines and traps. Robots in the military can be seen as positive or negative for humanity.

▲ Some people argue that robots and humans can live together happily and that robots are a positive thing for humanity.

The Ethics of Artificial Intelligence

Artificial intelligence has many **ethical** issues that experts have to consider. Currently, humans program robots and computers with the information and behaviors that they want them to learn. It is argued that one day these machines may be so advanced that they no longer listen to what humans want and, instead, make their own decisions based on their own **logic**. For example, if humans consider the problem of the world food shortage, the most obvious solutions seem to be to increase food production around the world or reduce consumption in some countries so that other countries have more. To an AI computer, however, the most logical thing may be to reduce the number of humans in the world.

The study of machine ethics is concerned with how machines behave toward humans, as well as toward other machines. One problem faced by **ethicists** is that ethics is about right and wrong and people's views on right and wrong can be different, depending on their individual values.

▼ Some people think that robots and computers with artificial intelligence may one day have the power and ability to take over the world and destroy humans.

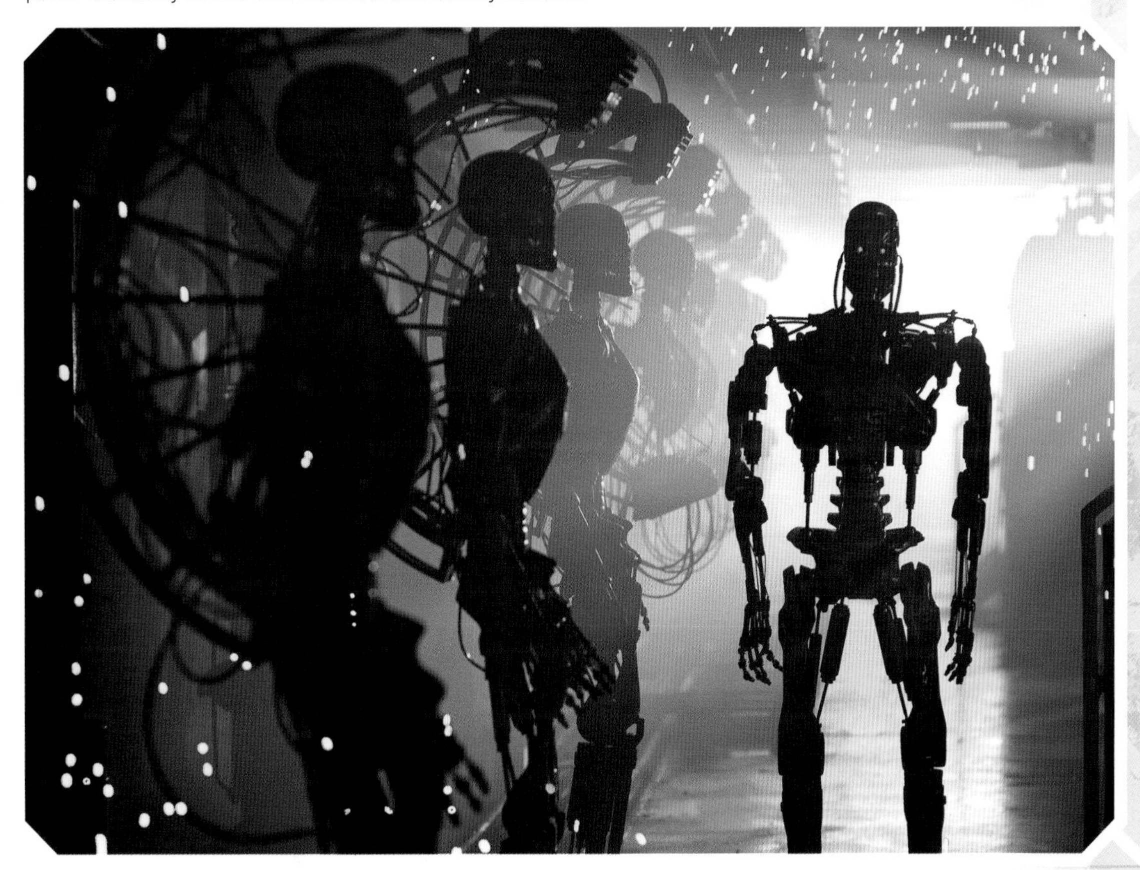

Robot Ethics Charter

The government of South Korea has drawn up a Robot Ethics Charter. It gives guidelines for ethical rules to be programmed into robots so that they do not harm humans—but the charter also protects robot "rights" so they are not abused.

True Artificial Intelligence?

The ultimate aim of many AI experts is to produce a program or machine as close as possible to the human brain. In 1637, however, the French mathematician and philosopher Rene Descartes predicted that it would never be possible to make a machine that thinks exactly as humans do.

ethical to do with what is right and wrong

ethicists people who study ethics

logic system of reasoning, which involves thinking, understanding, and forming judgements, considering all the facts and possibilities

What Does the Future Hold for Robots and Artificial Intelligence?

When it comes to technology, predicting the future is extremely difficult. However, it is safe to assume that in the future some robotics and artificial intelligence technologies will be much smaller, help out in the home, help the environment—and engage in warfare.

Nanorobots

Nanorobotics is the field of technology that is trying to create **devices** that are as small, if not smaller, than a **nanometer**. These objects are called nanorobots.

Nanorobotics would have particular value in the field of medicine. Nanorobots could be injected into the human body and used to treat illnesses or injuries. It could be possible to treat cancer by injecting nanorobots that would hunt down and destroy cancer cells. These nanorobots could be fitted with a tiny camera, drugs to be delivered to the affected part of the body, a power source, and a tail to help with movement and changing direction.

Microrobots

At the moment, the smallest robots are known as microrobots. They are less than 0.1 of an inch (2.5 mm) in length and width but, compared to a nanorobot, they would be like elephants standing next to an ant.

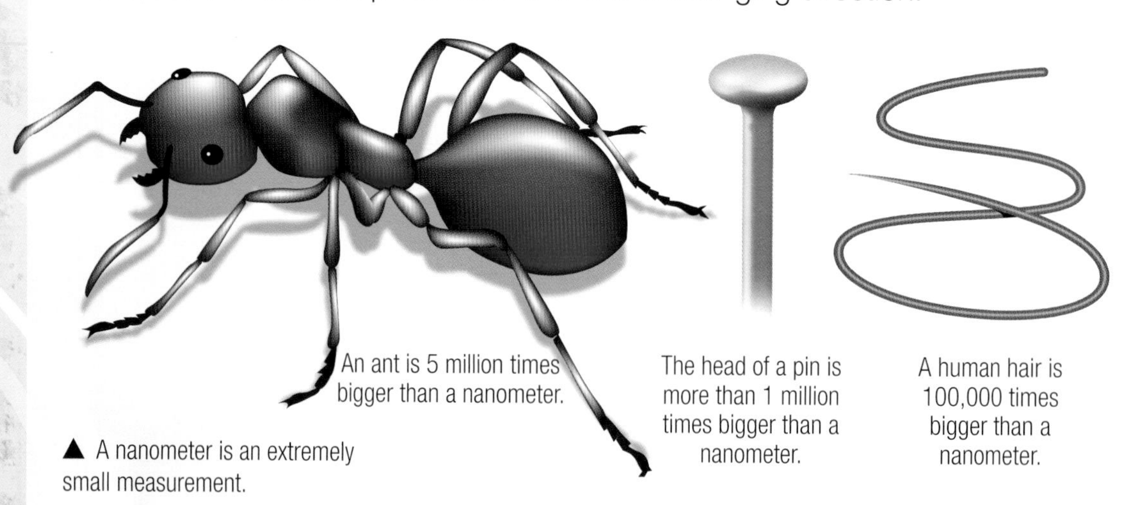

▲ A nanometer is an extremely small measurement.

Word Watch

devices things made for a particular purpose or to do a particular job

nanometer measurement equal to one billionth of a meter or one millionth of a millimeter

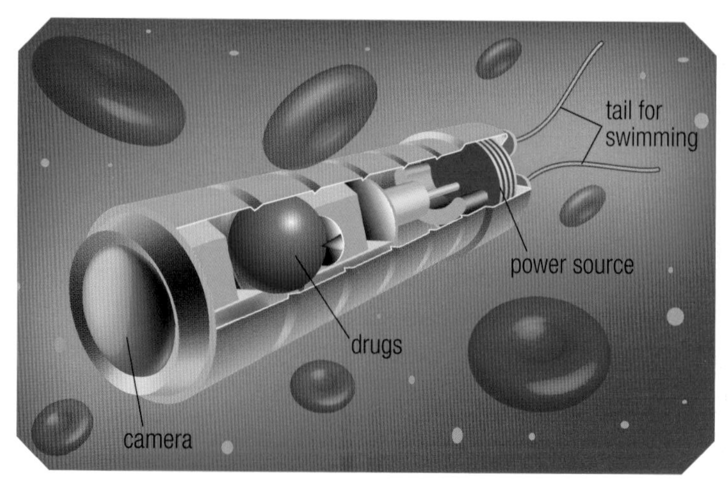

▶ Nanorobots could swim through the bloodstream and deliver drugs to the site of infection or disease.

Web Watch

www.sciencemuseum.org.uk/antenna/nano/skin/index.asp
www.nanozone.org

Helping Out at Home

Many robotics and AI experts believe that in the future households will have robots that help them with daily chores. Already, there are robotic vacuum cleaners and washing machines. These could be joined by robots that act as maids and butlers.

▲ In the future, people might get robots to do chores and help them in the home.

Robots and the Environment

One of the biggest issues for humankind is looking after the environment and finding new, clean ways of producing electricity. Robotic technology can help. Already, scientists in Britain are developing a robot that eats live slugs and produces electricity from their **decomposing** bodies. The name of the robot is Slugbot!

Military Robots

Robotics and AI will play an increasingly important role in the military. The U.S. military has a study, called Project Alpha, that is examining how to develop robots that are capable of replacing humans on the battlefield and performing **combat** functions.

Da Vinci's Robots

It is not just modern scientists who have studied robotics. Drawings of robots by the artist, scientist, and mathematician Leonardo da Vinci have been discovered. He drew these robots more than 500 years ago.

Word Watch

combat fighting

decomposing decaying, rotting, and breaking down

Index

A

actuators 9
AERCam Sprint 19
Afghan Explorer 18
agricultural robots 10, 11
AIBO 22
Amazon.com 27
artificial intelligence 5, 24–5, 26–7, 28, 29, 30, 31
artificial limbs 16, 17
ASIMO 8, 22, 25
Asimov, Isaac 6
Astro Boy 23
Automated Guided Vehicles 10
autonomous robots 6, 12, 20, 21

B

BattleBots 21

C

C-3PO 7
Capek, Karel 6
Clarke, Arthur C. 23
computer scientists 5, 24
controller 8

D

Dante II 18
da Vinci, Leonardo 31
Data, Lieutenant Commander 23
Deep Blue 26
Deep Drone 8000 18
deep-sea exploration 11, 18
degrees of freedom (DOF) 10
Delta robots 15
Descartes, Rene 29

E

educational robots 10, 11
ethical issues 12, 29
expert systems 25

F

facial recognition system 24, 25
fuzzy logic 27

G

Gates, Bill 4

H

handwriting recognition system 25
human brain 12
humanoid robots 10, 11, 13, 19, 22, 24, 25

I

industrial robots 10, 14–15

L

learning systems 25
LEGO Mindstorms 22
Logic Theorist 25

M

medical robots 10, 16–17
microrobots 31
military robots 28, 31
mobile robots 10

N

nanorobots 30
National Aeronautics and Space Administration (NASA) 19
neurons 12, 17, 26
Newell, Allen 25
Nomad Rover 18
Noo Noo 7

O

Oracle 11

P

Pyramid Rover 18

R

R2-D2 7, 23
Raibert Hopper V 22
RoboCup 20
Robonaut 19
Robot Ethics Charter 29
Robot Hall of Fame 22–3
robotic surgery 16
Robot Rumbles 21
Rotterdam Docks 14, 15
Russell, Andy 13

S

Sandbot 9
SCARA 22
science fiction 7, 23
sensors 8, 10, 13, 19, 27
Shadow Hand 9
Shakey 22
Simon, Herbert 25
six-axes robots 15
Slugbot 31
Sojourner Rover 19, 22
space exploration 18, 19

T

T-800 7
telerobots 10, 11
telesurgery 15
Turing Test 26

U

Unimate 10, 22

V

voice recognition software 27